Published by Creative Education and
Creative Paperbacks
P.O. Box 227, Mankato, Minnesota 56002
Creative Education and Creative Paperbacks
are imprints of The Creative Company
www.thecreativecompany.us

Design by The Design Lab
Production by Dana Cheit
Art direction by Rita Marshall
Printed in the United States of America

Photographs by Alamy (Mark Conlin, Reinhard
Dirscherl, Doug Perrine, Jamie Pham, Photononstop),
Dreamstime (Lukas Blazek, Wrangel, Zepherwind),
iStockphoto (ArnonPolin, DaddyNewt, IMNATURE,
jordieasy, semet, sipaphoto, tonaquatic), Shutterstock
(Eric Isselee)

Library of Congress Cataloging-in- Publication Data
Names: Bodden, Valerie, author.
Title: Seahorses / Valerie Bodden.
Series: Amazing Animals.
Includes bibliographical references and index.
Summary: A basic exploration of the appearance,
behavior, and habitat of seahorses, the small,
snouted fish of the oceans. Also included is a story
from folklore explaining how seahorses became fish.
Identifiers: ISBN 978-1-64026-040-5 (hardcover) /
ISBN 978-1-62832-628-4 (pbk) / ISBN 978-1-
64000-156-5 (eBook)

This title has been submitted for CIP processing under
LCCN 2018938941.

CCSS: RI.1.1, 2, 4, 5, 6, 7; RI.2.2, 5, 6, 7, 10;
RI.3.1, 5, 7, 8; RF.1.1, 3, 4; RF.2.3, 4

AMAZING ANIMALS

SEAHORSES

BY VALERIE BODDEN

CREATIVE EDUCATION • CREATIVE PAPERBACKS

Seahorses are not horses at all. They are fish! There are more than 50 kinds of seahorses. Scientists are still finding new ones!

Lined seahorses (above) and Pacific seahorses (right) are just two kinds

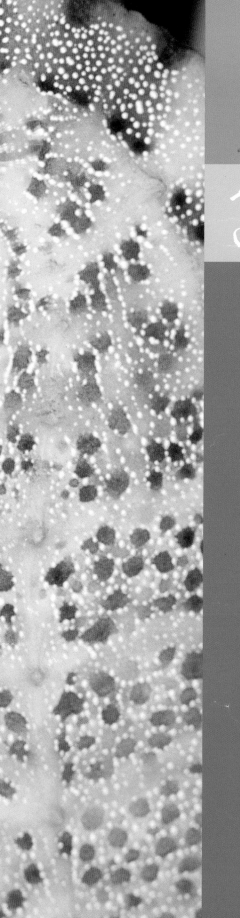

The small fin on a seahorse's back flutters up to 35 times per second

A seahorse body is long and thin with small fins. It has a long snout and big eyes. The seahorse uses its long tail like a hand. It grasps sea plants or **corals**. Seahorses can be many colors. Some seahorses can even change color! This helps them blend in with their surroundings.

corals tiny sea animals with tube-shaped bodies; their skeletons harden to form coral reefs

The biggest seahorses can grow up to 13 inches (33 cm) long. The smallest seahorses are the size of a bee! Seahorses swim upright. This makes them slow. Some can swim only about five feet (1.5 m) in an hour.

One type of pygmy seahorse (right) is about 1.1 inches (2.7 cm) long

Seahorses hang on to coral (opposite) and grasses (left) with their tails

Most seahorses live in the ocean. They like warm, **shallow** water. Many live in areas with lots of seagrass. Others live on **coral reefs**.

coral reefs ridges of rock in the sea made by the skeletons of coral

shallow not deep

Seahorses eat

zooplankton. They can eat more than 3,000 zooplankton a day! Seahorses have no teeth. They suck up zooplankton with their snouts.

zooplankton tiny animals that float in the ocean and other bodies of water

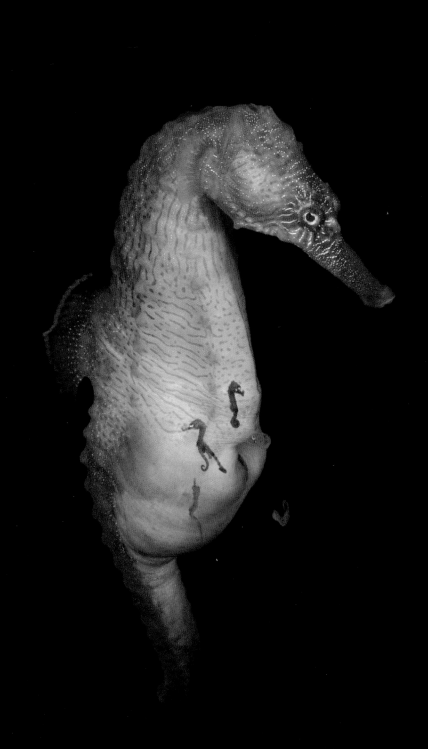

A male's brood pouch holds the eggs while they change into fry

Female seahorses do not have babies. Males do! **Fry** develop in a pouch on the male's belly. He may carry hundreds or thousands of young at a time! Newborn fry are tiny and almost clear. They live on their own. Only a few survive to adulthood. Seahorses live one to five years.

fry baby seahorses

Most seahorses live alone or in pairs. But some live in groups called herds or colonies. Seahorses do not move far from where they were born.

Long-snouted seahorses may move to deeper waters in the winter

*Pacific seahorses do a
good job of hiding in
the Sea of Cortez*

Seahorses spend their days clinging to plants or coral with their tails. They stay still. This way **predators** like fish and crabs will not see them. The seahorses snatch any zooplankton that float by.

predators animals that kill and eat other animals

Seahorses are hard to spot in the wild. But lots of aquariums (*uh-KWARE-ee-ums*) and zoos keep seahorses. It can be fun to see these odd-shaped creatures up-close!

Seahorses may not have scales like other fish, but they do have gills

A Seahorse Story

Why is the seahorse a fish? People in Mexico told a story about this. Long ago, all animals wore clothes. Seahorse was a land animal then. One day, he played a prank on the other land animals. The animals chased Seahorse toward the sea. Seahorse pulled off his sandals. He looped them in his belt. Then he ran into the water. Seahorse grew small fins where his shoes had been. He became a fish.

Read More

De la Bédoyère, Camilla. *My Little Book of Ocean Life*. Lake Forest, Calif.: QEB, 2016.

Uttridge, Sarah, ed. *Ocean Animals Around the World*. Mankato, Minn.: Smart Apple Media, 2015.

Websites

Enchanted Learning: Seahorse
http://www.enchantedlearning.com/subjects/fish/printouts/Seahorsecoloring.shtml
This site has seahorse facts and a picture to color.

PBS: Kingdom of the Seahorse
http://www.pbs.org/wgbh/nova/seahorse/
Learn more about seahorses.

Note: Every effort has been made to ensure that the websites listed above are suitable for children, that they have educational value, and that they contain no inappropriate material. However, because of the nature of the Internet, it is impossible to guarantee that these sites will remain active indefinitely or that their contents will not be altered.

Index